11773 7722

THE CHEROKEES

Also by Elaine Landau

Alzheimer's Disease

Black Market Adoption and
the Sale of Children

Colin Powell: Four-
Star General

Cowboys

Dyslexia

Endangered Plants

Jupiter

Interesting Invertebrates:
A Look at Some Animals Without Backbones

Lyme Disease

Mars

Nazi War Criminals

Neptune

Robert Fulton

Saturn

The Sioux

Surrogate Mothers

Tropical Rain Forests
Around the World

We Have AIDS

We Survived the Holocaust

Wildflowers Around the World

ELAINE LANDAU

THE CHEROKEES

FRANKLIN WATTS
A Division of Grolier Publishing
New York London Hong Kong Sydney
Danbury, Connecticut

Map by Joe LeMonnier
Cover photograph copyright ©: Ron Sherman
Photographs copyright ©: Artworks/Jerry Sinkovec: pp. 10, 11; New York Public
Library, Picture Collection: pp. 14, 21, 36, 37, 46, 51; National Museum
of the American Indian: pp. 3, 15, 19, 25, 26, 28, 29; Photo Researchers, Inc.:
p. 24 (Roberto De Gugliemo/SPL), 30 (Porterfield/Chickering), 39 (Tom McHugh/
Cal. Acad. of Science); Historical Pictures Service, Chicago: pp. 40, 44;
Woolaroc Museum, Bartlesville, Oklahoma: p. 47; Unicorn Stock Photos: p. 50
(Martha McBride); Kent & Donna Dannen: p. 52.

Library of Congress Cataloging-in-Publication Data
Landau, Elaine.
The Cherokees / by Elaine Landau.
p.   cm.—(A First book)
Includes bibliographical references and index.
Summary: Discusses the history, customs, and current situation of
the Cherokee Indians.
ISBN 0-531-20066-3
1. Cherokee Indians—History—Juvenile literature.   2. Cherokee
Indians—Social life and customs—Juvenile literature.
[1. Cherokee Indians.   2. Indians of North America.]   I. Title.
II. Series.
E99.C5L3   1992
970.004'975—dc20   91-30262   CIP   AC

FRANKLIN WATTS
A Division of Grolier Publishing
Sherman Turnpike
Danbury, CT 06813

CONTENTS

THE CHEROKEES

LONG AGO...

It was the golden autumn of the year. Everyone in the Indian village prepared for an important celebration. They burned their old clothing and worn household items. They aired out possessions they wanted to keep and scrubbed their homes.

In a few days, they would take part in the Friendship Ceremony, *Atohuna*. This celebration granted each person the chance for a fresh start in life. It was a time to forget old grudges and errors. A new sacred fire was lit in the Council House at the village center. People gathered embers from this special flame to rekindle the fires that burned within their own homes.

During Atohuna, the people drank a dark-colored fluid to cleanse their bodies. For a week they took part in tribal dances. These dances symbolized kindness, friendship, and love. Now everyone looked forward to the future. They hoped for good fortune and honor.

CHEROKEES IN TRADITIONAL GARMENTS
PERFORM TRIBAL DANCES DONE BY THEIR
ANCESTORS HUNDREDS OF YEARS AGO.

These were the Cherokee Indians. Before white people ever landed on America's shores, these Indians inhabited the mountains and valleys of an area that included parts of what is now Tennessee, North Carolina, South Carolina, Virginia, West Virginia, Kentucky, Georgia, and Alabama.

The large Cherokee nation was made up of numerous Indian villages. These were usually built near rivers and streams, which provided fresh water and trout to the tribe.

Although the Indian villages varied in size, they were similarly arranged. At the center of a Cherokee village, often on higher ground, stood the Council House. Here important meetings were held. Near to both the Council House and the river was a flat area called "the Square." Celebrations, ceremonial dances, and public games were conducted there. There were also tribal community gardens and a grain storehouse. At the outer edge of the village stood a *stockade* built of tall wooden posts. This structure provided protection from any surprise enemy attacks.

Surrounding the village were the homes of Cherokee families. These windowless wooden dwellings were plastered both inside and out with a mixture of clay and grass. They had thatched roofs made of tree bark.

Inside the homes were brightly colored woven rugs and beautifully made baskets. There was also bedding

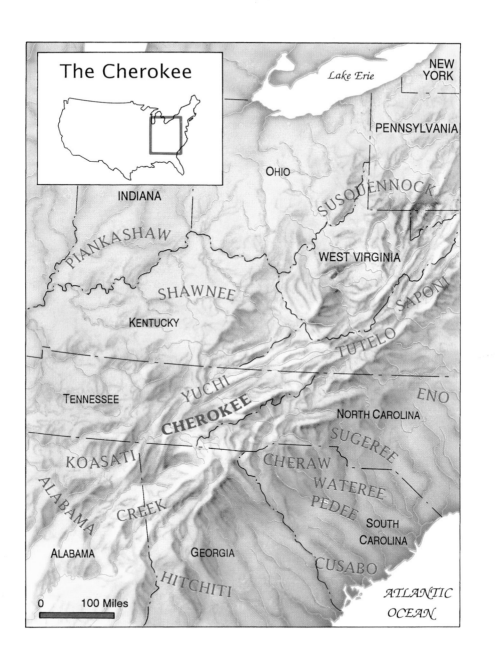

The Cherokee

THIS PICTURE TAKEN IN 1926 SHOWS A CHEROKEE WOMAN
WEAVING A BASKET IN FRONT OF HER HOUSE. THE EARLY
CHEROKEES ALSO HAD WOODEN HOUSES.

A BEAUTIFULLY WOVEN
CHEROKEE BASKET. NOTICE
ITS ATTRACTIVE DESIGN.

for the family as well as cane seats fashioned from tree bark. A fire blazed in each home's center. The smoke went out through a small hole in the roof. Near the fire stood a round stove for baking bread.

On cold winter nights, the family often slept in a nearby dugout called a *hothouse*. To provide warmth, a fire continually burned in this small, earth-covered structure. Some special ceremonies took place in the hothouse. Here the Cherokees often shared tribal stories and legends with their young. Through them, Cherokee children learned about their people—one of the largest and most respected tribes in the southeast.

DAILY LIFE

The Cherokee nation consisted of seven clans, or large family groups. Among these were the Bird, Wolf, and Deer clans. Other clans were the Wild Potato Clan, the Long Hair Clan, the Blue Clan, and the Paint Clan. Members of all seven clans lived in every Cherokee village. A child was born into his mother's clan. He received his identity within the Cherokee nation through her.

Cherokee women enjoyed a good deal of power. They were free to choose the men they wished to marry. Following the wedding, a Cherokee husband either went to live in his wife's mother's house or built a new house for his bride. The house, as well as any children born to the couple, belonged to the woman.

Although Cherokee women were highly regarded, they still did a good deal of work. Women cooked the meals and cared for the home and the children. A Cherokee woman gathered nuts, mushrooms, berries, and roots from the wooded areas surrounding her village. She also raised vegetables for her family. Corn, called *sele* by the Cherokees, was an important crop for the tribe. Women and their daughters planted and harvested crops in their allotted community garden plots.

Cherokee women performed numerous other tasks as well. They tanned animal hides to make clothing. They made deerskin shirts and *breech clouts* for the men to wear in the summer. For the winter they made warmer clothing out of buckskin and animal furs. The women made their own deerskin summer skirts as well as buffalo garments for the colder months. They also produced large squares of woven material which both Cherokee men and women would wrap around their bodies.

A woman's brothers trained her sons in the tasks performed by Cherokee men. Men made blowguns, bows and arrows, *tomahawks,* and canoes. They fashioned hooks from animal bones to catch fish from nearby rivers and streams. Cherokee Indians were also excellent hunters. Using blowguns, bows and arrows, spears, and traps, they hunted deer, elk, rabbits, wild turkeys, squirrels and other animals.

Tribal Government ➤ The vast Cherokee Nation was governed by a central body. In turn, each village had its

THIS COLORFULLY WOVEN SHOULDER BAG WAS AMONG
THE GARMENTS MADE BY CHEROKEE WOMEN.

own government patterned after the nation's. Every village had a chief. Two men, known as the right-hand man and the speaker, helped him to rule. Both sat next to the chief in the Council House. Six other men, led by the right-hand man, also assisted the chief in important tribal matters and decisions. During peacetime, these men conducted ceremonies, held court, and made laws.

However, when the Cherokees were at war, another chief, called the *kalanu,* along with his counselors, took charge. The war chief wore red, whereas the peace chief dressed in white.

Some Cherokee women—those who had won honor through a heroic act—also had a role in tribal government. These women would often help plan battle strategies as well as decide whether a war prisoner should be executed or made a tribal member.

War ➛ Although the Cherokees preferred to live in peace, they were known for their courage in facing enemies. Victory in battle was extremely important to a Cherokee. Defeat could mean death or torture. There was always also the possibility of being captured and sold into slavery by the winning tribe.

Cherokees learned to be prepared for battle. Portions of their land had also been claimed by other tribes. And in years to come, white settlers would find Cherokee territory extremely desirable as well.

CHIEF STALKING TURKEY WAS A CHEROKEE CHIEF
KNOWN FOR HIS BRAVERY AND WISDOM.

Before going to war, the Cherokees performed war dances and songs. Frequently they knew exactly when and where to strike an enemy. This is because Cherokee spies wearing various animal skins were sent out in different directions ahead of the others. When one of the spies spotted the enemy, he would make the noise of the animal whose skin he wore. That way the others knew in which direction to advance.

Warrior training began early on. Many young boys were given limited quantities of food. It was hoped that by learning to live with hunger, they would develop such important warrior traits as will power and endurance.

Brave warriors wore an eagle feather as a symbol of their courage. However, before a boy could earn his feather, he had to perform difficult feats in front of other tribal members. He also had to win honor in battle.

Religion ➡ The Cherokees were a spiritual people. Many objects within nature held deep religious meaning for them. *Yowa,* called the creator by today's Cherokees, was the supreme power they worshiped. The Cherokees believed that Yowa created the earth for everyone. During the day, he allowed the sun to govern, while at night the moon ruled. Yowa created fire to help his people survive; through its smoke their prayers were carried up to him.

Priests or medicine men performed religious rituals

and marriages. They were skilled in using herbs and barks for healing. Quartz crystals, which were sacred to the Cherokees, were also used by medicine men. Priests did not hunt or fish with the other village men. Instead, they lived on what they earned for their services. A medicine man held a powerful position within the tribe. He was honored and respected.

Crafts ➥ The Cherokees were skilled *artisans*. Using shells, bones, feathers, and seeds, they fashioned beautiful jewelry and hair ornaments. They used clay from the earth to make jars, pots, and bowls. These containers were used for daily cooking and carrying out tasks as well as for storage. Especially decorative jugs were also sometimes used in religious ceremonies.

Many Cherokees were expert carvers. Cherokee men created pipes, canoes, hunting and cooking tools, and other items out of materials found in nature, such as stone and wood. The Cherokee Indians were perhaps best-known for basket making. Using honeysuckle vines, river cane, and wild hemp, Cherokee women wove beautifully designed baskets. They painted the baskets with dyes from such plants as the blood root, yellow root, and others.

Games, Dance, and Music ➥ Throughout the year, the Cherokees celebrated seven major festivals with feasts,

CHEROKEE MEDICINE MEN USED QUARTZ CRYSTALS,
SUCH AS THE ONES SEEN HERE, FOR HEALING.
(FACING PAGE) THE CHEROKEES FASHIONED AN
ASSORTMENT OF JUGS AND JARS FOR BOTH
CEREMONIAL AND EVERYDAY USE.

CHEROKEE MEN CARVED FINELY
DESIGNED PIPES SUCH AS
THE ONE SHOWN HERE.

songs, and dances. These celebrations marked such events as the first new moons of spring and autumn, different stages of the corn's growth, and other important times in the lives of the people.

The Cherokees celebrated the hunt with the Beaver and Raccoon Dances. The dancers acted out killing and skinning the animal as well as tanning the hides. During a Buffalo Hunt Dance, men and women wore buffalo masks and copied the animal's movements. A favorite animal dance of the Cherokees was the Bear Dance. Bears were greatly respected by Cherokee hunters. According to Cherokee legend, long ago bears were humans.

A Cherokee ball game, *anetsa,* played between men from two Cherokee towns, was also a major event. In this game, teams won points for hurling a ball past a goal post, using sticks shaped like small tennis rackets. At times these games became quite rough. Players might be kicked, hit, and even scratched by opposing team members.

Another popular game among the Cherokees was called *tsung-ayi unvi.* In this game, a smooth stone disk was rolled across the square. The players who chased the object threw poles wherever they thought the disk would land. The player whose pole was closest won points. The Cherokees used this game to help young boys develop their spear-throwing skill. Feasting, dancing, and music often accompanied these sporting events.

HAND-CARVED MASKS SUCH AS THESE WERE USED
IN VARIOUS TRIBAL CEREMONIES.

THE CHEROKEES MADE GOURDS INTO MUSICAL INSTRUMENTS.

The Cherokees made a number of musical instruments. From hollowed-out sections of tree trunks, they fashioned water drums, which were stained with red clay or various berry juices. The Indians also carved beautiful wooden flutes. They used gourds from their gardens to make rattles. These instruments were played as dancers whirled in a circular motion around the village square.

THE WHITE SETTLERS' ARRIVAL

The arrival of white people in the New World dramatically changed the Cherokees' way of life forever. At first there were only small groups of trappers and settlers. Often they approached the Cherokees in peace. However, as time passed, the numbers of whites greatly increased. It soon became clear that these individuals were more interested in the Cherokees' land than in their friendship.

New settlers cleared the area's timberlands to make way for their own farms. They plowed fields, built cabins, and fenced off large portions of land. As the whites established settlements along important river sites, the Indians' fishing and hunting areas began to vanish. Before long, game had grown scarce.

The Indians tried to curb the white colonists' invasion peacefully, but their pleas were ignored. Even though a number of treaties had been signed to protect

Cherokee rights, these promises were soon broken. Realizing that the settlers' greed for land meant more than their word, the Cherokees fought to keep their way of life. A series of bloody skirmishes between Cherokees and whites resulted.

By 1776, the time of the American Revolution, the Cherokees had learned not to trust the pioneer settlers who had stolen their lands. Instead, they joined forces with the British, hoping to defeat the colonists. British soldiers and Cherokees attacked settlements in South Carolina, Georgia, and Virginia.

The frontier settlers ruthlessly fought back. Frontiersmen rode into Cherokee villages shooting everyone in sight. They set fire to Indian cabins and food storehouses. The destruction of Indian villages and loss of life soon became widespread. The Cherokees realized that further resistance was pointless. The whites would surely slaughter their people.

When Cherokee leaders asked the whites for peace, it was granted only in return for even more of their land. In addition, white agents now oversaw the Cherokees to be certain they were not preparing to attack again.

During this difficult period, the Cherokees did their best to survive. To some degree this often meant taking on the ways of the whites. Without woodland hunting areas, the Cherokees increasingly turned to farming and cattle raising. They planted and spun cotton and made maple sugar. Some Cherokees prospered. They owned sizable farms and orchards with large numbers of cows, horses, and hogs.

Yet most Cherokees did not fare as well. The Indians worked extremely hard, but they were given nearly nothing by the whites in exchange for what they produced. For example, in return for a bushel of corn or vegetables, a Cherokee woman might receive only a petticoat or a small container of salt. Although the treaties with the whites had promised the Cherokees cattle and such farming equipment as plows and hoes, these were rarely received.

Yet the Cherokees continually proved themselves to be adaptable and resourceful as a people. One brilliant Cherokee named Sequoyah devised a Cherokee alphabet to provide his tribe with a written language. It took Sequoyah twelve years to create eighty-five symbols to represent the spoken Cherokee language. In 1821 his alphabet was adopted by the tribal chiefs. The Cherokees soon became the only American Indian tribe to read and write in their own language.

Word of Sequoyah's impressive accomplishment spread. He had won the respect of both his own people and the whites. This influential Cherokee, along with a group of other Indian leaders, traveled to Washington, D.C., to speak for his people.

AFTER WHITE SETTLERS TURNED CHEROKEE HUNTING
GROUNDS INTO FARMS, SOME CHEROKEES STILL PROSPERED.
MAJOR RIDGE (SHOWN HERE) HAD A LARGE FARM ON
WHICH HE GREW COTTON AND CORN. HE LATER RAISED
HORSES, CATTLE, AND HOGS.

SEQUOYAH, INVENTOR OF THE
CHEROKEE ALPHABET, WAS OFTEN
SEEN WEARING A TURBAN AND
SMOKING A LONG-STEMMED PIPE.

These leaders explained that to provide space for the whites, the Cherokees had been forced to sign nearly two land treaties a year. With each treaty they lost more of their territory. Even land not covered by these treaties was frequently forcibly taken by white settlers. Unfortunately, the Cherokees' journey to the white nation's capital resulted in little benefit to their people.

Meanwhile, several new developments made Cherokee land more desirable than ever. It was learned that abundant amounts of iron ore and silver lay untapped on Indian property. In 1828, when a small Indian boy sold a gold nugget to a trader, the whites thought that Cherokee territory might be rich in gold as well. There had also been reports of valuable stones found there. However, as the Indians believed these stones should never be sold, they kept them out of the reach of white traders.

Prompted by greed, the white settlers pressured the Cherokees to leave the region. They wanted the Indians to journey west to the portion of land in Oklahoma that had been parceled off as "Indian Territory." At times, the whites even defied their own courts of law to take additional Indian land. For example, following the discovery of gold on Cherokee property in Georgia, the state decided to add this area to its own holdings. The United States Supreme Court upheld the Indians' claim to the region. However, the white settlers simply refused to honor the Court's verdict.

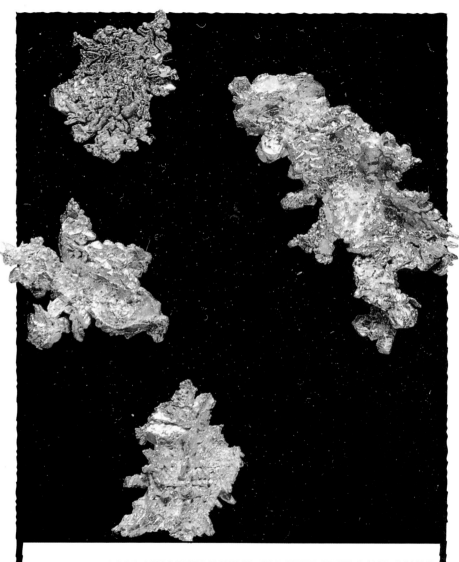

STORIES OF GOLD NUGGETS FOUND ON CHEROKEE LAND MADE
THE INDIANS' PROPERTY EVEN MORE DESIRABLE TO WHITES.

HERE CREEK CHIEF RED EAGLE SURRENDERS TO ANDREW JACKSON.
ALTHOUGH THE CHEROKEES FOUGHT WITH THE WHITE SOLDIERS
AGAINST THE CREEKS, JACKSON LATER REFUSED TO LET
THE CHEROKEES REMAIN ON THEIR LAND.

President Andrew Jackson, who had formerly lived on the frontier, dealt harshly with the Cherokees. His actions reflected his own bigotry and ungratefulness. Years earlier, when Jackson fought against the Creek Indians, he had sought the Cherokees' aid. Chief Junaluska had sent five hundred men to help Jackson win in battle.

In fact, during the Battle of Horseshoe Bend, Junaluska saved Jackson's life when a Creek warrior was about to kill him. Thirty-three Cherokees died that day on the battlefield, and many more were wounded. But Andrew Jackson lived to later wholeheartedly support the forced removal of the Cherokees to the West. Even when Chief Junaluska personally pleaded with Jackson to protect his people, Jackson told him that nothing could be done for them.

Some journalists and congressmen did their best to defend Indian rights, but their outcry wasn't strong enough to curb the country's anti-Indian feelings. It soon became clear that a treaty provision which provided for the removal of the Cherokees by May 1838 would be enforced.

THE TRAIL OF TEARS

A wise Cherokee leader once said, "If we had no land, we should have fewer enemies." The harsh truth behind his words became especially clear in one of the most shameful episodes of our nation's history.

On May 10, 1838, General Winfield Scott of the United States Army ordered his men to forcibly take the Cherokees from their homes. Four thousand soldiers, assisted by three thousand volunteers, were used to separate these peaceful people from their land.

The soldiers hoped to catch the Cherokees off guard. Divided into small bands, they quietly crept into the tribe's Smokey Mountain region. There they arrested every Cherokee man, woman, and child in sight. Men were pulled from the fields; their wives and children were dragged from their cabins. All were forced to walk to the stockade with the sharp point of a soldier's bayonet only inches from their backs.

DESPITE HIS BRUTAL TREATMENT OF THE CHEROKEES,
GENERAL WINFIELD SCOTT BECAME A DECORATED WAR HERO.

Once the stockade was filled, the Indian captives were loaded onto wagons in which they would be transported west like livestock. The Indians had not been permitted to bring warm clothing for the long and often freezing journey ahead. Some people had even been taken from their cabins barefooted.

It was terrifying to be rounded up at gunpoint by soldiers whose language you didn't understand. In one instance, a band of soldiers barged into a home in which a small child had died only the day before. There, a group of women had been preparing its tiny body for burial. The soldiers took the child's mother and other women away before the child could be buried.

In another, nearby cabin, a woman and her four small children were hurriedly ushered out in much the same way. The mother had strapped her infant to her back as she led the other children from the cabin. But the strain proved too much for her. She fell on the way to the stockade, and died of an apparent heart attack with her infant still strapped to her body.

Witnessing these horrors, some Cherokees tried to flee from the soldiers, and many of them were shot. Others managed to safely hide out in the mountains.

Meanwhile, the removal continued. A procession of wagons brimming over with its human cargo began to roll westward. As the wagons pulled away, hundreds of tear-stained faces could be seen. Young children trembled as they waved good-bye to their pets and homes.

TAKCHEE WAS A CHEROKEE GUIDE FOR U.S. TROOPS AT THE
TIME OF THE CHEROKEE REMOVAL. DESPITE THE LOYAL
SERVICE PROVIDED BY MANY CHEROKEES, THEIR PEOPLE
WERE STILL FORCIBLY TAKEN FROM THEIR HOMES.

ON THE SHAMEFUL JOURNEY WEST KNOWN AS THE TRAIL OF TEARS,
SOLDIERS CRUELLY HERDED THEIR CHEROKEE CAPTIVES ACROSS
COUNTRY AS THOUGH THEY WERE CATTLE.
(*THE TRAIL OF TEARS* BY ROBERT LINDNEUX)

The long journey to Oklahoma's "Indian Territory" proved to be a merciless ordeal for the Cherokees. They either slept in the wagons or on the cold, hard ground. They did not have a fire for warmth or even a thin blanket to cover them at night.

Having to cope with poor treatment, scant food supplies, and brutal weather, large numbers of Cherokees became extremely ill. Often, more than twenty Indians were found dead each morning.

At one point during the journey, a chief's wife offered her cloak to a sick, shivering child. Now she only had a thin summer dress to wear in the freezing sleet and snow. Before long, the woman developed pneumonia. When her husband was unable to wake her one morning, he realized that she had died during the night.

She, along with the others who had perished, was buried in a shallow unmarked grave along the trail. There had been no time for religious rites or prayer. The Cherokee removal had to be completed in under three weeks.

The soldiers showed little mercy for the elderly or disabled. One morning a man in his nineties who was nearly blind had difficulty climbing up into a wagon. To force him to move faster, a soldier lashed him with a bull whip.

The long pain-filled trip to Oklahoma finally ended on May 26, 1839. Four thousand Cherokees had died along the way. The journey became known as the Trail of Tears.

THE CHEROKEES TODAY

The Cherokees who escaped the soldiers' roundup remained out of sight in the mountains of western North Carolina. There they survived as best they could living quietly in the hills and forests. Since Indians were not permitted to own land, sympathetic whites purchased some areas for the Cherokees to use.

Eventually laws were passed which recognized these Cherokees as United States citizens. The land they lived on then became known as the Cherokee Reservation, or the Qualla Boundary. Now this area legally belongs to the tribe.

There are about 8,500 Cherokees in the East. Nearly 3,000 of these people have chosen not to live on the *reservation*. Cherokees living on the reservation still have a chief and a tribal Council House where they meet to settle tribal issues.

There are five elementary schools and one high

THIS YOUNG GIRL DRESSED IN TRADITIONAL CLOTHING
AND THESE CHEROKEE GRANDPARENTS SHOW HOW THE
CHEROKEES HAVE CONTINUED AS A PROUD PEOPLE.

SKILLED CHEROKEE ARTISANS STILL
CREATE BEAUTIFUL BASKETS.

school on the reservation. Reservation children are not required to attend these schools. If they wish, they may go to a public school in the area.

Also, nearly 50,000 Cherokees live in the West. Cherokee life in Oklahoma differs from that in North Carolina. Oklahoma Cherokees no longer have a reservation. They also speak a different *dialect* of the language.

The Oklahoma Cherokees have a tribal government and have developed special programs to help tribe members economically. Many of the children are bilingual—they speak both English and their native language.

Today many Cherokees in both the East and West are anxious to achieve success in the mainstream of American society. These individuals are also interested in keeping the old ways alive. Numerous Cherokees are proud of their heritage and take part in their tribe's ceremonial life.

Some Cherokee craftspeople have won national recognition for their traditional Cherokee carvings. Other Cherokee artisans take pride in their tribe's traditional jewelry making. Their work is a present-day reminder of the beauty of their people's past and their potential for the future.

GLOSSARY

Anetsa   Cherokee ball game

Artisan   one skilled in arts and crafts

Atohuna   a friendship ceremony that was held by the Cherokees every autumn

Breech clout   a piece of cloth worn (by men) around the hips and thighs

Dialect   a variation of the standard language of a particular people

Hothouse   a sizable hole in the ground with an earth-covered framework; a fire was kept burning within a hothouse for warmth.

Kalanu   the Cherokee chief who took charge of the tribe during wartime

Reservation a tract of land set aside by the government for Indian use

Sele the Cherokee word for corn

Stockade a strong, high barrier made of posts or stakes, which was used for defense

Tomahawk a stone ax attached to a wooden handle used as a war weapon

Tsung-ayi unvi a popular Cherokee game involving spear throwing

Yowa the supreme power worshiped by Cherokees in their ancient religion

FOR FURTHER READING

Gammell, Stephen. *Dancing Teepees*. New York: Holiday House, 1989.

Goble, Paul. *Beyond the Ridge*. New York: Bradbury, 1989.

———. *Dream Wolf*. New York: Bradbury, 1990.

Lepthien, Emilie U. *The Mandans*. Chicago: Children's Press, 1989.

Wheeler, M. J. *First Came the Indians*. New York: Macmillan, 1983.

Yolen, Jane. *Sky Dogs*. New York: Harcourt, 1990.

INDEX

ABOUT THE AUTHOR

Elaine Landau has been a newspaper reporter, a children's book editor, and a youth services librarian. She has written over thirty-five books for young people. Ms. Landau makes her home in Sparta, New Jersey.